Thankful Roots

Book 5 Reflections of God Moments
56 One Minute Devotionals

Dedication

Roots are the first part of the plant that establishes it and allows it to grow and flourish into the true purpose and plan of what the plant should be. I have been very blessed to have strong roots grown through the hardest of times by watching and experiencing the truth of God in my parents' lives. I do not know a stronger nor more God-fearing couple. Through life's ups and downs, they have held me up and supported me. They have always directed me back to the One in whom I am rooted. To my mom and dad who have truly been all that life could ask for in parents and who have truly helped me to become rooted in Him. Don and Teresa White, you are my heroes and the example of who I want to be when I grow up!

Thankful Roots
Book 5 Reflections of God Moments
56 One Minute Devotionals
copyright © 2024

All rights reserved. No part of this book may be reproduced or utilized in any form or by any means, electronic or mechanical, including photocopying, recording, or by any information storage and retrieval system, without written
permission from the publisher.

All Scripture quotations are taken from The Message, copyright © 1993, 2002, 2018 by Eugene H. Peterson. Used by permission of NavPress. All rights reserved. Represented by Tyndale House Publishers.

Scripture taken from the New King James Version®. Copyright © 1982 by Thomas Nelson. Used by permission. All rights reserved.

Written by: Donesa Walker
Design by: Will Baten

Table of Contents

1. Steady Buzz!
2. The Coming Day!
3. Bone Deep!
4. Seasoned!
5. Amazing Grace!
6. Glowing!
7. Panting!
8. Knocking!
9. Wise Discipline!
10. Cool It!
11. Yielded!
12. Channels!
13. Comments of Thought!
14. Duck!
15. Marvels!
16. Working At Relationships!
17. The Point of Snow!
18. Mirror Mirror!
19. Permit It!
20. Stinkin' Thinkin'!
21. Happiness Is!
22. Privilege!
23. What Is Man?
24. Ask!
25. Rest!
26. Plans!
27. The Mission of Market!
28. Refusal To Love!
29. Marathon of Life!
30. Glial Growth!
31. Purpose Through The Pain!
32. Why Evil?
33. Perspectives!
34. Uniqueness!
35. Hot Air!
36. Too Much!
37. Rooted!
38. What Are You Seeking?
39. The Great Commandment!
40. Your Plan!
41. Beauty!
42. Leaning In!
43. Pondering!
44. Timelines!
45. Better Than Chocolate!
46. Outer Vessel!
47. Gate Opener!
48 Prudence!
49. Substitutions!
50. Knit Together!
51. Contingency!
52. Warning: This Is A Sermon!!!
53. Pile Up!
54. Thankful Heart!
55. A Worry Through!
56. Steady Rejoicing!

Jesus answered by quoting Deuteronomy: "It takes more than bread to stay alive. It takes a steady stream of words from God's mouth."

Matthew 4:4

Steady Buzz!

What a beautiful picture of this bee at work gathering what it needs to produce honey and feed its family. The thing is that for this worker bee, it is working to achieve for the whole not for itself and just by doing its work, it pollinates our fruit, veggies, flowers, etc. Sometimes we become too fixated on our own problems, dilemmas and situations that we fail to understand that the purpose for our lives is bigger than us alone or our agenda. Jesus instructed those before him and through them, us...that it is in the steady stream of His words where life is found. It's not a one time thing nor an occasional thing but a steady thing. You see this honeybee understands that he must continually work in a steady manner to achieve the tasks set before him.

There aren't "off" days. There may be off days to your job or your career but there is never an off day in your marriage nor your parenting nor your loving nor your serving nor your relationship with Christ. It's not a drip from a faucet that takes forever to fill up on nor a filled up tub that you can just go grab some stagnant water from...it's a steady stream of His wisdom and love that fills you. It's not a Sunday fill up then empty out all week...it's a steady outpouring from Him that keeps life everlasting flowing through you. Are you feeling clogged up, gummed up with the cares of this world? Are you allowing the pressures of the job or the stress of living to make you beat down?

Come to the steady stream of His love. It's rich and filling. It will begin to flow over you and allow Him to unclog your spirit and be refreshed. I love Spring because it reminds me that He makes all things new. Even the flower dying from wintery harshness has purpose in Him and still has new life to give. Lord, help me to freshen myself in your steady stream of love and grace. Allow me to be a vessel of purpose working for your glory today.

Blow the trumpet in Zion;
sound the alarm on my holy hill.
Let all who live in the land tremble,
for the day of the Lord is coming.
It is close at hand—
a day of darkness and gloom,
a day of clouds and blackness.
Like dawn spreading across the mountains
a large and mighty army comes,
such as never was in ancient times
nor ever will be in ages to come.
"Even now," declares the Lord,
"return to me with all your heart,
with fasting and weeping and mourning."
Rend your heart
and not your garments.
Return to the Lord your God,
for he is gracious and compassionate,
slow to anger and abounding in love,
and he relents from sending calamity.

Joel 2: 1-2, 12-13

The Coming Day!

My heart is heavy today as God has impressed upon me that the time is coming where war is all many will know. I awoke in a cold sweat after a terrible vision of the outpouring of His wrath upon America for her refusal to help those in need. It hurts my heart to think of the fear and trauma many will endure but there is a way of escape, a beacon of hope. Jesus is coming for His bride, the church. He says to turn towards Him with all your heart and He will have mercy and relent. Lord. I come in humble repentance asking you to turn your anger from our land. I know we have done so wrong to the innocent and downtrodden and for this I cry for your mercy.

I see the pictures of a war torn country of Ukraine as Russia tears at them like a bear but I also know your mercy and forgiveness is true and real. I hear the alarm and am sounding it for others to hear....your day is at hand. I ask you for mercy on our country for our failures.

The Lord appeared to us in the past, saying:
"I have loved you with an everlasting love;
I have drawn you with unfailing kindness.

I will refresh the weary and satisfy the faint."

"This is the covenant I will make with the people of
Israel after that time," declares the Lord.
"I will put my law in their minds
and write it on their hearts.
I will be their God,
and they will be my people.

Jeremiah 31: 3 ,25, 33

Bone Deep!

Bone deep weariness wears on a body, mind & soul. Sorrow and physical maladies come at you and can beat you down. But God made a covenant of love through Jesus Christ that is everlasting. The law has become the law of love. You see love cannot do someone wrong...not God's love. His love completely satisfies...that's what satiated means. His love is so complete that it clears out the weariness, sorrow & depression with His fullness. The truth is that most of us don't take the time to walk in His complete love. It's a choice. It's like a cup under a flowing faucet...His love is overflowing and always there. If you are down and your spirit is weary, put your cup of life into the flow of his living water of love.

Allow him to supply, fill and satisfy you so you may once again be His hands extended. Then pour out and refill constantly as a vessel of His anointed. He desires to replenish you. Lord, fill me today with your love, to overflowing so that I may be a vessel of yours to flow into the lives of others drawing them to your fountain of love.

Continue earnestly in prayer, being vigilant in it with thanksgiving;

Walk in wisdom toward those who are outside, redeeming the time. Let your speech always be with grace, seasoned with salt, that you may know how you ought to answer each one.

Colossians 4: 2, 5-6

Seasoned!

Yesterday I went to lunch with a friend to celebrate her birthday and she seasoned me with her approach of redeeming the time towards our waiter. She carefully and cautiously approached him in speech and after engaging him, inquired about his knowledge of Jesus. She was vigilant and earnest and thankful. It blessed me so. Our relationship with Christ and with others should be a flowing experience of His love. Our gifts are each as unique as our mission field of ministry where He has placed us. He provides the resource in words, Spirit and prompting. We are to be yielded and vigilant so that in our walk of wisdom we understand the moments He has opened and are able to season the moments with His love. The instructions in this verse are from the Spirit of God through Paul to the church from his prison cell.

Never before in history has it been so important for us to walk carefully in grace redeeming the time as it is swiftly fading. Knowing how and when to answer and respond to those in need is more urgent as our time is short. The day of the Lord is at hand and we know not the hour that He comes but we can see the signs in the world and the groaning can be felt in the Earth and our spirit senses the urgency. If today was the very last day that you could win someone to God, who would you contact? Why are you waiting?

This is the message which we have heard from Him and declare to you, that God is light and in Him is no darkness at all. If we say that we have fellowship with Him, and walk in darkness, we lie and do not practice the truth. But if we walk in the light as He is in the light, we have fellowship with one another, and the blood of Jesus Christ His Son cleanses us from all sin.

1 John 1: 5-7

Amazing Grace!

A friend posted this picture that she took in a field that she was walking through at night. She said she had a flashlight but the low clouds/fog alone reflected the cross. Some people will look at it and say well it's really just the power pole in the fog because I can see the wires...which is what brings me to the point. Perception. If we say we are walking in light but the darkness hides within us...we are lying to ourselves and others. The danger in this is more than just the lie. The danger is of allowing that darkness to grow by hiding it. That darkness can be resentment or bitterness or hidden sin. Time to clear the fog so that the perception is clearly seen.

I love this picture of the cross...it reminds me of His plan for me. Lord, I thank you for the cross. I thank you for the price you paid. I thank you for washing all my sins away and that you came. I thank you for your amazing grace. I thank you for life. I thank you, for all!

Repent therefore and be converted, that your sins may be blotted out, so that times of refreshing may come from the presence of the Lord,

Act 3: 19

Glowing!

This opportunity presented by this beautiful picture only occurs because of an algae that is bioluminescent. It is the evidence of the algae doing its job. Hebrews tells us that faith is the substance of things hoped for and the evidence of things not seen. To one, this is a picture of faith. It shows the washing and the refreshing that the tide brings to the shore. Think of this in our lives. Are we bioluminescent in the things we do for Christ? Can those around us see the evidence of our repentance and refreshing? Are we glowing with the light of Christ reflecting in our very being? Lord, wash me in your refreshing so that I may shine your light to others. I repent of all my wrongdoing both those things intentionally done and unintentionally. I ask that you wash me anew today in your refreshing so that I can be a light that shines brightly drawing others to your presence. Do not let me be clouded with doubts and fears but rather to walk confident in your presence. I thank you for your work in my life and I willingly surrender all to you.

As the deer pants for the water brooks,
So pants my soul for You, O God.
My soul thirsts for God, for the living God.
When shall I come and appear before God?

Deep calls unto deep at the noise of Your waterfalls;
All Your waves and billows have gone over me.
The Lord will command His
lovingkindness in the daytime,
And in the night His song shall be with me—
A prayer to the God of my life.

Psalms 42: 1-2, 7-8

Panting!

Right now, we recognize the desperation & resolve in the faces, voices and messages of the Ukraine people. David when writing this song also felt the desperation for God's intervention in his situation. His deep well in his heart called out for the waterfall of God's love to fill him and he compared his desperation for God to the desperation of a deer panting in need of water...you see a deer running needs water for thirst quenching but also safety as it hides the scent from dogs chasing. When we come to God in desperation, He is there as the constant waterfall of love hiding us from our enemies and quenching our undying thirst. He is our source. Our desperation doesn't have to be a crisis. Being desperate for God can be a mindset. Desperation is a strong desire. The prayer of this psalmist was for a song in the night.

A song that brought peace in the midst of crisis and a day filled with God's loving kindness was the cry of his heart. Lord, I am desperate for you. Not because of my situation only but because my heart desires you above all others. Help me to focus on you and on your purposes for my life. Let me bathe my life in your loving kindness so that I may extend the same to those around me. Make me like you Lord.

Behold, I stand at the door and knock. If anyone hears My voice and opens the door, I will come in to him and dine with him, and he with Me. To him who overcomes I will grant to sit with Me on My throne, as I also overcame and sat down with My Father on His throne.

Revelation 3: 20-21

Knocking!

With so much ongoing in Ukraine and heightened concerns here from those who grew up in the Cold War & RED DAWN....this verse is so apropos. Christ is saying Look to Him. He's standing at the door knocking, waiting to come dine with us. Overcomers and Conquerors are who dine with Him. He's coming and knocking...isn't it time you answered? Do not let fear overtake you. He instructs us that the birds of the field know His voice and know he cares for them. How much more is He aware of our situation and our need?

The rod and rebuke give wisdom,
But a child left to himself brings shame to his mother.

Correct your son, and he will give you rest;
Yes, he will give delight to your soul.
Where there is no revelation, the people cast off restraint;
But happy is he who keeps the law.

The fear of man brings a snare,
But whoever trusts in the Lord shall be safe.

Proverbs 29: 15, 17-18, 25

Wise Discipline!

God's Wisdom is from God and God is wise. He instructs us here through the wisdom of Solomon to discipline our children and ourselves. But fear of human opinion will keep you from trusting God and will keep you undisciplined. Our eyes cannot see what He is doing nor His purposes. But if we attend to what He wants….our eyes are opened to His way and His plans. When we get alone with Him and discipline ourselves to His ways and acknowledge His will upmost in our lives… then He reveals to us His plan and guides us. God is delighted when His children are disciplined in their lives by spending time in His presence and in His word. These canyons of beauty were not formed instantly but rather through the endurance of weathering. The rocks were sheared away through beatings of other things against their surface and fast running floods of water tearing through that valley. The storms that come through there work a thing of beauty but the storm itself isn't pretty.

Lord, help me to remain steadfast in you. Disciplined to your word and open to your vision. Let my spiritual eyes see what you have In front of me so that I may go forth. I trust in you with all my heart. Help me to remain steadfast in you, unmovable by man's opinions that are not aligned with your word and who you are. I know the coming storms are scary but I know they work a thing of beauty in me when I trust in you. Thank you for your sweet peace in the valley of the storm and your continuing presence in my life.

Be sober, be vigilant; because your adversary the devil walks about like a roaring lion, seeking whom he may devour. Resist him, steadfast in the faith, knowing that the same sufferings are experienced by your brotherhood in the world. But may the God of all grace, who called us to His eternal glory by Christ Jesus, after you have suffered a while, perfect, establish, strengthen, and settle you. To Him be the glory and the dominion forever and ever. Amen.

1 Peter 5: 8-11

Cool It!

Oh my spirit just could not get quiet last night as I prayed fervently for the people across the world in the Ukraine especially who are crying out to God. You see, God raises up intercessors who will pray when you are in distress. I don't know exactly who I prayed for nor their specific need as I prayed in the Spirit through His groaning and uttering. This may sound strange to some but part of being the hedge around others is willingness to lose sleep. Our finite mind wants peace and safety here on this flawed planet but that will never be for we live in a world tainted with sin. The Devil wants the church to lay down much like others do in the face of destruction but we are over-comers who need to rise up. This morning I am reminded of Samson...who took the jawbone of a donkey and slew thousands. Our jawbone is our weapon and we are to use it to proclaim God's word and to pray in intercession for those who cannot for God hears and he controls the heads of governments, armies, and all that is in earth. Miracles happen when we believe. Stay strong! Pray! Jesus is coming soon...signs of these times are everywhere!

Seek the Lord while He may be found,
Call upon Him while He is near.
Let the wicked forsake his way,
And the unrighteous man his thoughts;
Let him return to the Lord,
And He will have mercy on him;
And to our God, For He will abundantly pardon.
"For My thoughts are not your thoughts,
Nor are your ways My ways," says the Lord.
"For as the heavens are higher than the earth,
So are My ways higher than your ways,
And My thoughts than your thoughts.
"For as the rain comes down, and the snow from heaven,
And do not return there, But water the earth,
And make it bring forth and bud,
That it may give seed to the sower
And bread to the eater,
So shall My word be that goes forth from My mouth;
It shall not return to Me void,
But it shall accomplish what I please,
And it shall prosper in the thing for which I sent it.

Isaiah 55: 6-11

Yielded!

Sometimes I'm fascinated that the science of weather is so wrong...one of the only jobs where you can be wrong badly and still be easily forgiven is a weatherman because we understand the principle that nature is fickle and changes. God isn't fickle and He controls the weather. He set things in motion when He said Let there be light, thousands of years ago and these things still proceed forward. His mind and heart isn't limited by what we see/feel but He understands us because His son came and dwelt among us. He desires to lavish his love and forgiveness on us but we must be willing to yield to his ways for his ways are higher than ours as they see the whole picture. His words have power and purpose that will be achieved. He compares his word to rain that waters the ground. That rain has purpose and doesn't return to the sky until it has done what it was sent to do. Think on that for a minute.

God gave each raindrop a job to achieve before it can return to heaven. Think if he gave a raindrop purpose, then he certainly has a purpose for you. If you wonder what your purpose is, it is to be light. It is to be His hand extended to others. What are you doing to achieve your purpose? If you don't know...it's time to seek him and ask of him to define your purpose in him. Lord, I thank you that each of us has purpose in you and you did not send us without a job to accomplish.

Help me Lord to always find my purpose in you by seeking your will in my life.

The king's heart is in the hand of the Lord,
Like the rivers of water;
He turns it wherever He wishes.

He who follows righteousness and mercy
Finds life, righteousness, and honor.

Whoever guards his mouth and tongue
Keeps his soul from troubles.

There is no wisdom or understanding
Or counsel against the Lord.
The horse is prepared for the day of battle,
But deliverance is of the Lord.

Proverbs 21: 1, 21, 23, 30-31

Channels!

When a friend posted a picture of the flowers popping up in the yard in the midst of winter, I couldn't help but think of the words of wisdom scattered throughout scripture especially in Proverbs. If we will apply these words to our lives, we will be better for it. I like to find scriptures and put them onto index cards so that I can reflect on them each morning! I put them on my mirrors in my house so when I look at myself, I see His word. I like to put them on my walls for they remind me who He is...I like to surround myself with them for they give life! What is popping up in your yard of life today? Is it something fragrant and beautiful that will draw others to God? If not, it might be time to weed your garden of life of the things that distract and prepare the soil for growth through Him then surround your heart/life with His word so it can take root and grow something beautiful and fragrant in the midst of winter.

Lord, help me to be fruitful and fragrant no matter my circumstances! Help me to be what you would have me to be no matter my situation. Let your fragrance and your beauty shine through my life even in my winter moments.

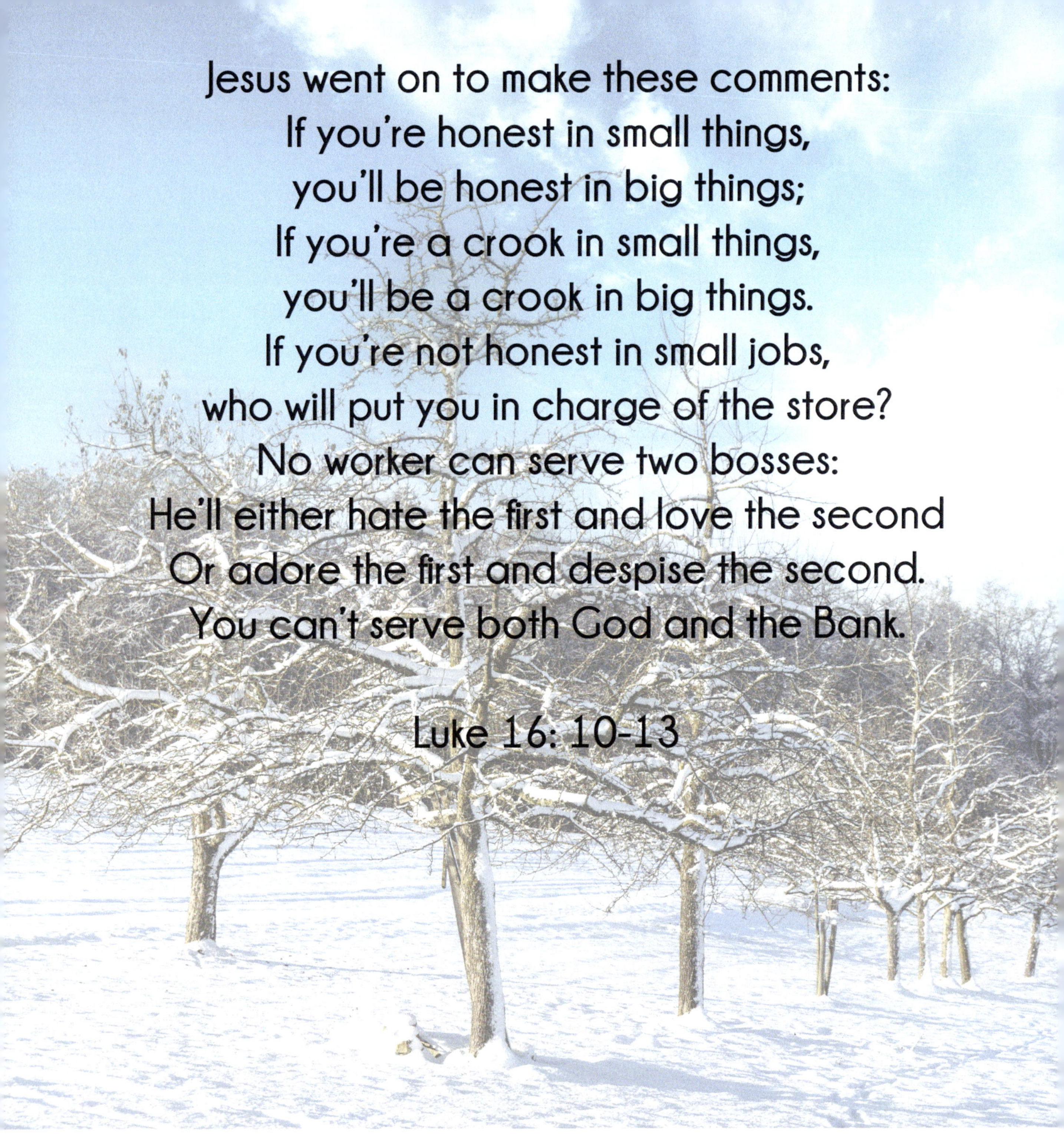

Jesus went on to make these comments:
If you're honest in small things,
you'll be honest in big things;
If you're a crook in small things,
you'll be a crook in big things.
If you're not honest in small jobs,
who will put you in charge of the store?
No worker can serve two bosses:
He'll either hate the first and love the second
Or adore the first and despise the second.
You can't serve both God and the Bank.

Luke 16: 10-13

Comments of Thought!

Thinking on this...pondering it because there is a truth in devotion. In my business, most of my employees work other jobs also. This really puts an important twist on me to do a good job as a boss to help them feel valued and appreciated as they are. Brain training takes passion and full attention. By serving my employees who serve my clients, everyone ends up happy. This verse says that a person cannot serve two bosses and love both which could be true in cases of measuring how bosses treat you. This is most particularly a heart issue. Jesus was saying that if a person works for monetary gain primarily and one job pays more than the other, resentment can build or if a person works for passion and feels abused by the place they serve, they begin to resent that. Finding balance in life is by aligning under His ways.

Jesus wants us to be of a servant's heart which means we desire to be as He was, serving others and leading them to God. As a boss, I want to serve my employees so that I lead by example. When I was a teacher for over 20 years, I had many bosses. I saw those who led by example and those who demeaned and distracted. The climate of the school was reflecting the person in charge. Being open and honest leads to openness and honesty in those around you. Leading by example...Lord, help me to be what you desire me to be in all things and in all places I serve. Help me to serve each person in my life as if I am serving you. Help me to be your hands extended reaching out to others.

"As the Father loved Me, I also have loved you; abide in My love. If you keep My commandments, you will abide in My love, just as I have kept My Father's commandments and abide in His love.

John 15: 9-10

Duck!

    I watched the ducks in the lake the other day and I saw a whole brood of ducklings who stayed in the trails their momma duck made. They stopped when she stopped and rested. They swam when she swam in her wake. They were completely at home in her care. I reflected that this is how God wants us to be. He wants us to be completely at rest in His care knowing that He is working out the best for us in this life and in eternity. Jesus instructed His disciples and all of us who choose to follow Him to make ourselves intimately at home in His love by keeping His commandments. I confess that I slept so well in my own bed last night. It's so good to be home even though spending time away was necessary. Being at home means you're at rest and relaxed. God wants us to feel at home intimately with His plans and care for us. But just like a journey, it is a place we arrive into. We must choose to be at home in Him and trust Him to provide ways when there seems to be no way.

    We must trust that His plans for our lives are good enough and safe enough that we let go of our way and begin to live fully and intimately in His way trusting that He cares for us enough to supply all that we need according to His ways and His riches. Lord, I confess that I often know that you can take care of my needs but fail to rely on the promise that you WILL! I get caught up in the "failures" of my wants and convince myself that when a dream or something I have worked at totters or when my health suffers or when a plan I had in my head doesn't thrive, that you have forgotten me.

    I ask for forgiveness for this weakness in me. I ask that you help me to have faith not only that you can move the mountains in my life but you Will move those mountains as I dwell intimately in your presence. Help me to remain at home in you and quit taking side trips mentally to other ways that are not restful. Make me more like you Lord.

Come, behold the works of the Lord,
Who has made desolations in the earth.
He makes wars cease to the end of the earth;
He breaks the bow and cuts the spear in two;
He burns the chariot in the fire.
Be still, and know that I am God;
I will be exalted among the nations,
I will be exalted in the earth!

Psalms 46: 8-10

Marvels!

    I truly needed to focus on this today with all that is going on in our world. Getting your sights set on God and not the politics or other that bombards really helps you breathe deeper. God doesn't want us carrying the weight on our shoulders. That's why He sent His son Jesus to bear our burdens and free us from this. Focusing on Him! This morning my left foot was really hurting and I looked at Wes as we left our hotel, he was carrying all the bags so that I didn't have any weight to bear. I thought then what an example of how Christ bears our burdens. Lord, today I give it all to you.

Work at getting along with each other and with God. Otherwise you'll never get so much as a glimpse of God. Make sure no one gets left out of God's generosity. Keep a sharp eye out for weeds of bitter discontent. A thistle or two gone to seed can ruin a whole garden in no time. Watch out for the Esau syndrome: trading away God's lifelong gift in order to satisfy a short-term appetite. You well know how Esau later regretted that impulsive act and wanted God's blessing—but by then it was too late, tears or no tears.

Hebrews 12: 14-17

Working At Relationships!

The truth is that, relationship is work whether it is a marriage or a friendship and if you don't work at it, it grows weeds. Weeds can choke out the good and leave a nasty experience that hurts all involved. A small seed of discontent leads to a patch of weedy bitterness. Esau grew a garden of regret because he sold out God's plan for him for a short term pleasure. We are often guilty of this. We push in an area that God isn't in or we get ahead of God's timing because we are in a hurry and we pay for it long term. God's not finished with us. He wants us to get along with others and with Him but our relationship with Him takes work too. We must invest the time with Him in order to truly know Him on a deeper level. God desires a close relationship and intimacy with us but intimacy takes investment of time and purpose.

Question of today: how am I investing into my relationships with God, spouse, children, friends, employees/employer? Am I being deliberate and purposeful or am I taking things for granted and growing hidden weeds that will soon choke my relationship? Am I investing purposefully? Watering, fertilizing and nurturing the growth I want to see? This picture is a waterfall at Yosemite but if you wait patiently, when the sun strikes it just right...it becomes a waterfall of fire. It requires the investment of time to experience it. Are you investing time patiently with those around you or are you selling your long term blessings short for a quick fix?

Now the purpose of the commandment is love from a pure heart, from a good conscience, and from sincere faith, from which some, having strayed, have turned aside to idle talk, desiring to be teachers of the law, understanding neither what they say nor the things which they affirm.

1 Timothy 1: 5-7

The Point of Snow!

Sitting here in Colorado watching the snow fall and cover the ground which yesterday looked muddy and ugly but today covered in a blanket of white looks beautiful! This is what is meant when His word says He washes us white as snow. He covers a multitude of our gunk with His wonderful presence and forgiveness. His sacrifice of love made Supreme atonement for all our sins. If you move the coverage away, the dirty in our world is still there but His love says our sin is removed as far as the east is from the west. Now if we don't choose to stay and live under His covering, then the muddy mess begins to pile on top of the beauty and turns it back into a muddy mess but this time it's harder to get traction because the ice has built up causing a slick spot.

I am so thankful for His mercy and His grace which washed me clean and washes me over and over from all the world splashes into my life. Love... greater love has no man than He who laid down His life for us!

But be doers of the word, and not hearers only, deceiving yourselves. For if anyone is a hearer of the word and not a doer, he is like a man observing his natural face in a mirror; for he observes himself, goes away, and immediately forgets what kind of man he was.

James 1: 22-24

Mirror Mirror!

Ever caught yourself in a mirror and for just a second thought who is that? This is how the Word compares those who do not act on God's word nor listen to His ways. God is always speaking to us but it is up to us to listen. His PA system of His word is evident and abounding everywhere but we must choose to tune in. Listening involves more than just the physical act of hearing. It also involves the action of doing what we heard. On Sunday, a message from the Lord came through the Spirit to press in. Specifically it said to not let our situations or stresses distract us from His purpose but to Press In to His purpose.

He has called us out of darkness into His marvelous light so we might catch a spark and light our world. What are you doing today to go light your world? Are you being a candle, a lighthouse, a floodlight? Are you drawing people in to His goodness? Lord, help me to be salt and light for those around me. Help me to so walk in your power that the bugs that bite me go away singing There's power in the Blood! Help me to be a light to someone's darkness today!

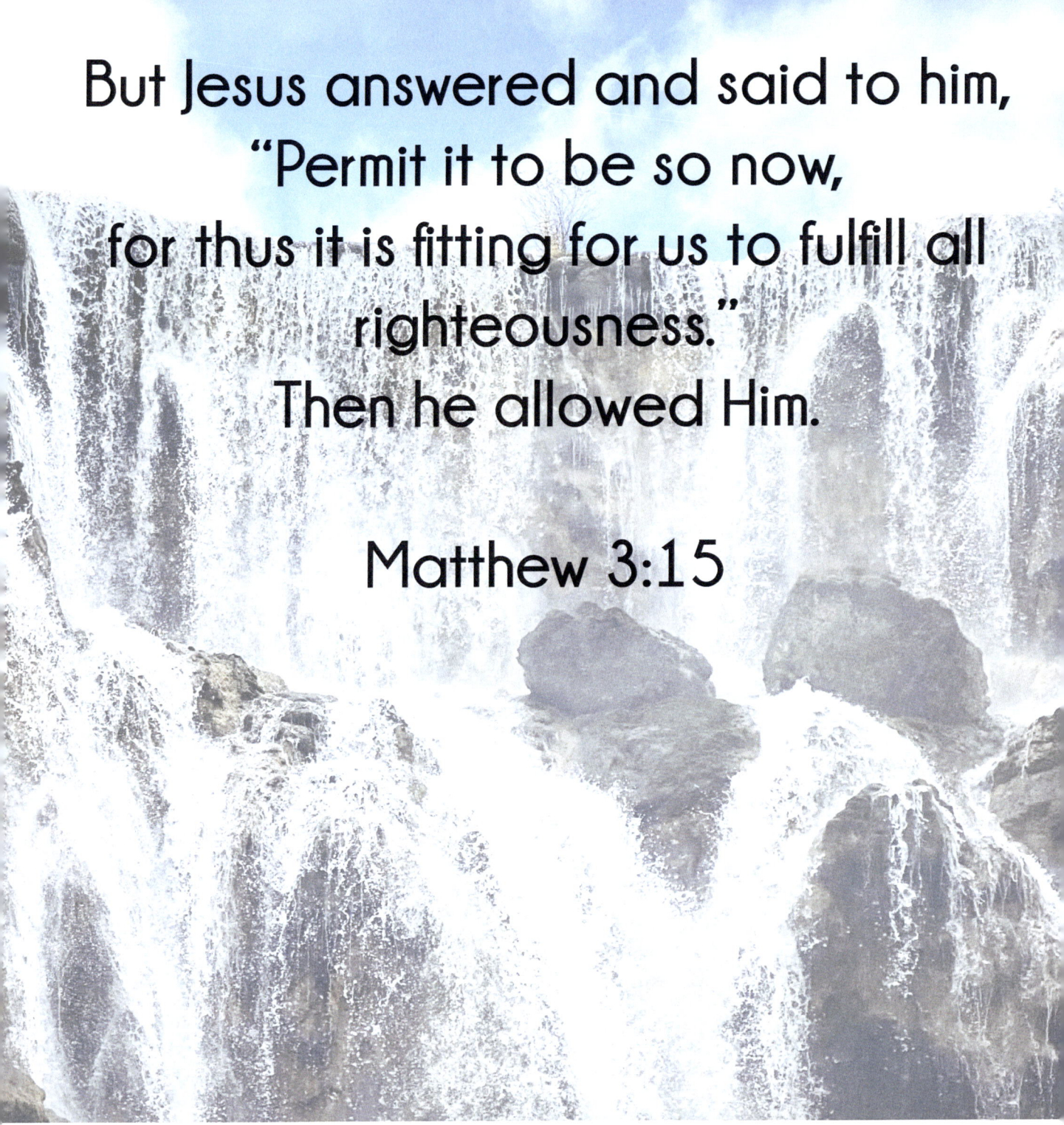

But Jesus answered and said to him, "Permit it to be so now, for thus it is fitting for us to fulfill all righteousness." Then he allowed Him.

Matthew 3:15

Permit It!

Reading this morning about John the Baptist and how Jesus himself followed the path of water Baptism in order to walk in His ministry. He instructed John to permit it, meaning that He wanted John to baptize Him. Jesus came to fulfill the law to the nth degree so that all prophecy would be fulfilled and He could be the sacrifice. Imagine the shock and awe when at His Baptism the voice of God Himself echoed across that place. Wow! But I want you to look at this exchange. I want you to see that God/Jesus/Holy Spirit are gentlemen. Jesus asked John for permission to be baptized by him and at the end of the verse, John allowed it.

This is how God works in our lives. He wants to work on your behalf but you must allow it for He desires to be with you but FOR NOW, He is calling tenderly. For now, He is the bridegroom preparing for His bride...the time is now to be a part of all He has to offer.

And do not be conformed to this world, but be transformed by the renewing of your mind, that you may prove what is that good and acceptable and perfect will of God.

not lagging in diligence, fervent in spirit, serving the Lord; rejoicing in hope, patient in tribulation, continuing steadfastly in prayer;

Do not be overcome by evil, but overcome evil with good.

Romans 12: 2, 11-12, 21

Stinkin' Thinkin'!

Get rid of your stinkin' thinkin' and let God refresh your mind. Yesterday I had a rough morning with things weighing heavily on my heart and mind. Honestly my body & emotions were run ragged and I just felt like a wreck. I encouraged myself in the Lord and thought I'm just going to go get my hair cut then go about my day but God....let me tell you that God met me at my hairdresser's stall. First, what is the chance that I walk in to get a haircut and I am the only one in the whole place on a Saturday? Never has happened in the 24 years I've been going there! Then Kim channeled God and spoke to me about Faith over Fear.

She encouraged me and challenged me and exhorted me and...well, Kim is Korean and sometimes hard to understand but every single word she spoke was so clear, concise and perfect. When I was growing up I was fascinated by the fact that God used ordinary people in ordinary situations to do amazing things. This is what I experienced yesterday and it has reinvigorated me to His way of thinking! I let the ways of the world get to me but then He met me and transformed me literally...she colored my hair too while we were talking so I have a new Do and a new hairdo! Thank you Jesus for meeting us where we are!

The preparations of the heart belong to man,
But the answer of the tongue is from the Lord.
All the ways of a man are pure in his own eyes,
But the Lord weighs the spirits.
Commit your works to the Lord,
And your thoughts will be established.

A man's heart plans his way,
But the Lord directs his steps.

He who heeds the word wisely will find good,
And whoever trusts in the Lord, happy is he.

Proverbs 16: 1-3, 9, 20

Happiness Is!

Happiness is... A few years ago, a marketing firm shared with me that the main focus of commercials was to depict happiness because that was what all people truly desired. They showed me many commercials and the primary focus was exactly that...projected happiness. Happiness is different from Joy. Joy is a fruit of the Spirit and flows from a deep place into others. It's contagious. Happiness is determined by our state of mind. Joy brings happiness but happiness exercised releases Joy. We are so caught up often in what others think, making plans to catch attention of someone else or wrapped into our own perception of self rather than living and walking in His light and path. God orders our steps and our contentedness of His path for us allows us to be happy. I love that old song ♪ Happiness is knowing my Savior, living a life in His favor, making a change in my behavior...Happiness is knowing the Lord. ♪♪

Commitment to His path, His way, leads to a state of mind focused on Him which is what happiness is. That complete trust and state of mind bears the fruit of Joy. My momma always told me that Joy stood for Jesus first, Others next and Yourself last to spell JOY. 𝄞Jesus, Others, & You what a wonderful way to spell Joy! Jesus, Others & You in the life of each girl and each boy. J is for Jesus for He has first place. O is for others we meet face to face and Y is for You and for all that you do. Put Jesus first, put others next, put yourself last to spell Joy! ♪

O Lord, You are my God.
I will exalt You,
I will praise Your name,
For You have done wonderful things;
Your counsels of old are faithfulness and truth.

For You have been a strength to the poor,
A strength to the needy in his distress,
A refuge from the storm,
A shade from the heat;
For the blast of the terrible ones is as a storm against the wall.

Isaiah 25: 1, 4

Privilege!

What a privilege it is to worship God with honor and praise knowing in confidence that He has planned such wonderful things for me! Even in my need, He is a tower of refuge! Stress weighs heavily on people in these days. It causes us to be overwhelmed and distracted from His purpose but in our distress and in our storms, God is there as a refuge and shelter. Lord, I want to run to you and physically feel you wrap me up in your loving arms. I know this metaphysical plane we are on leaves a lot to be desired but I am so appreciative that I can feel your presence and know that you are here with me. I pray a special covering of your mercy and grace in my situation that only you know. I pray for your provision and wisdom to walk the path set before me. I am so thankful for your constancy and faithfulness. Thank you for being my shelter in my storms:

Since they didn't bother to acknowledge God, God quit bothering them and let them run loose. And then all hell broke loose: rampant evil, grabbing and grasping, vicious backstabbing. They made life hell on earth with their envy, wanton killing, bickering, and cheating. Look at them: mean-spirited, venomous, fork-tongued God-bashers. Bullies, swaggerers, insufferable windbags! They keep inventing new ways of wrecking lives. They ditch their parents when they get in the way. Stupid, slimy, cruel, cold-blooded. And it's not as if they don't know better. They know perfectly well they're spitting in God's face. And they don't care—worse, they hand out prizes to those who do the worst things best!

Romans 1: 28-32

What Is Man?

A friend posted this picture of the horror that satellites are doing to our night sky. We as humans are filled with a desire for self. Without our Lord, we are consumed with all the things described in the verses below. But we have a Savior who willingly became the sacrificial lamb for us so that we might obtain mercy. God is a just God. He will not tolerate a proliferation of sin without repentance and He will abandon those who intentionally sin and lead others there with willfulness. They know God's ways and God's mercy & justice but choose to willfully sin. To these God has no tolerance...he sees them as He saw Sodom & Gomorrah. This chapter describes America in the willful embracing of sin and idolatry above all else even though Paul was describing Rome at the time he wrote these verses. God is merciful but God is also just. He sees those who know Him and He sees those who willfully turn from Him and lead others into the same.

In a world fraught with injustice, filled with lies & hate, reeling in a mire of sin...there is God. He is jealous of me. He desires me to be with Him. He wants the best for me and He will not tolerate sin. I am so thankful for His mercies. I am so thankful for His justice, his protection, His faithfulness to me. What is man that God is so mindful of him? I am His. Despite all flaws. He is mine and I am His. Wow! So powerful! Think on it. In a world filled with so much, the God of all creation thinks about me! How completely overwhelming and amazing!

"Ask, and it will be given to you; seek, and you will find; knock, and it will be opened to you. For everyone who asks receives, and he who seeks finds, and to him who knocks it will be opened. Or what man is there among you who, if his son asks for bread, will give him a stone? Or if he asks for a fish, will he give him a serpent? If you then, being evil, know how to give good gifts to your children, how much more will your Father who is in heaven give good things to those who ask Him!

Matthew 7: 7-11

Ask!

As I pondered on this scripture this morning, I couldn't help but think of how persistent my boys were when they were wanting video games. I knew gaming wasn't great for their lives so I was opposed for years and held out. They wrote essays to convince me and did anything I asked. They asked constantly and persistently. I knew every morning when I got up that they were going to bombard me with their request. I knew that gaming had some real drawbacks and I wanted to make sure they were old enough and mature enough to make good decisions in regards to this. I gave in to their requests even though I wasn't sure it was the right decision and am still not sure although it has brought some good things like new friends...It also brought some bad habits. My point is that God is the creator of all and He is omniscient. When we ask He knows what we need but His heart/mind can be moved. He is not a God without feelings nor a God without understanding of who we are.

He compares Himself to a parent whose heart is moved by His children. He wants only good for us. He knows His plan for us. His heart is for us and His eyes are on us. He is moved by us even when that isn't His original plan for us. He never plans for us to go off track and fall into situations not of His making but He is there for restoration when we are ready to come to Him humbly asking for forgiveness. He is for you. That's the most important thing to remember. When you are in pain or in the midst of a struggle and you feel alone because of choices of another or the weight of life...He is there and He is for you.

Therefore, since a promise remains of entering His rest, let us fear lest any of you seem to have come short of it. For indeed the gospel was preached to us as well as to them; but the word which they heard did not profit them, not being mixed with faith in those who heard it. For we who have believed do enter that rest, as He has said: "So I swore in My wrath,
'They shall not enter My rest,'"
although the works were finished from the foundation of the world. For He has spoken in a certain place of the seventh day in this way: "And God rested on the seventh day from all His works"; and again in this place: "They shall not enter My rest."
Since therefore it remains that some must enter it, and those to whom it was first preached did not enter because of disobedience, again He designates a certain day, saying in David, "Today," after such a long time, as it has been said:
"Today, if you will hear His voice,
Do not harden your hearts."

Hebrews 4: 1-7

Rest!

Rest. True rest free of worry, stress, fear and strife is hard to come by in this world fraught with the spirits of fear and chaos roaming about causing havoc. God's promise of rest is better than a good night's sleep or that boneless relaxation after a good massage. God's rest isn't a thing you only experience after you die either. God's rest is a place of pure contentment and peace. It is a place of total trust. I can tell you that I am one of those who tend to carry my worries, stress and tension in my body until I remember His words...come unto me all you who are weary and heavy laden...and I will give you rest...take my yoke upon you...hear me and be blessed...God's rest is a place we choose to enter but we must drop the earthly worries at the door for they have no part there. I love a good night's sleep because it is so necessary for the body/brain....but God's rest doesn't have to wait until I sleep. His rest is complete and open to the believer to enter and stay.

Whenever I go flying I have a pass to enter those special lounges sponsored by the airlines with the plush seats and quiet atmosphere. It's like stepping into an oasis in the middle of chaos. To me, that is just a small example of what God's rest is. It's a place of complete release and it is readily available to the believer. Lord, I am going to lay these burdens down now and step into your rest. The weights of all the world have gotten to me and I need your presence to refresh me and renew me. I want to lounge in your presence this morning before I start this day of ministry in my marketplace. Thank you that your yoke is easy and you carry my burdens for me so I can walk in your rest.

For thus says the Lord: After seventy years are completed at Babylon, I will visit you and perform My good word toward you, and cause you to return to this place. For I know the thoughts that I think toward you, says the Lord, thoughts of peace and not of evil, to give you a future and a hope.

I will be found by you, says the Lord, and I will bring you back from your captivity; I will gather you from all the nations and from all the places where I have driven you, says the Lord, and I will bring you to the place from which I cause you to be carried away captive.

Jeremiah 29: 10-11, 14

Plans!

Plans...something we make but if we are not listening to God's direction... the Israelites had been sent into captivity for their refusal to hear God. He had plans for them...then a oft misquoted verse is there...For I know the plans I have for you...good plans for a future and a hope...followed by the most important phrase... I will be FOUND by you. You cannot find something you are not seeking. The terms of their captivity led them back to the place of seeking God. He kept them in captivity for 70 years...a lifetime...a time of seeking that made reflection of the mighty miracles by the elderly stories to whet the appetite of the young. America has been spiraling downward in an "it's all about me" path for a long time. Abortion is rampant, killing and harming others has become a way of life for many. Television and talking heads on SM and our idol phones have stolen sacred time away from our families and our churches. We rarely see the miracles and signs now because we have become fat on our own ways...but God has allowed this time to define the true seeker...the believers who desire God above all else...those who teach their young to honor God, seek Him and He WILL be FOUND!

Signs of the times are everywhere and there is most certainly a feeling in the air of anticipation of His coming. Scripture tells us to be alert and ready for He comes as stealthily as a thief in the night. Why? Because He comes to claim His bride, His beloved...the ones who are seeking for by them He will be Found. Lord, the more I seek you, the more I find you. The more I seek you, the more I love you. I don't want to sit at your feet, I want to crawl up in your lap and lean on you to hear your heart. I want to be where you are. My desire is to Find you! Crush me in your presence. Wrap your arms of life and love around me. Help me to seek you above all else. Help me to rest in your embrace and know you are my God. I know we are led thru times of struggle to refine us but you know the plans for us. You know what you have set in store. Open my eyes that I may see your promise and that I may continue in your path.

Dishonest scales are an abomination to the Lord,
But a just weight is His delight.

The integrity of the upright will guide them,
But the perversity of the unfaithful will destroy them.

The righteous is delivered from trouble,
And it comes to the wicked instead.

The desire of the righteous is only good,
But the expectation of the wicked is wrath.
There is one who scatters, yet increases more;
And there is one who withholds more than is right,
But it leads to poverty.
The generous soul will be made rich,
And he who waters will also be watered himself.

Proverbs 11: 1, 3, 8, 23-25

The Mission of Market!

It's the small things that we set in our heart but God still sees! This morning I woke up to 2022 likes in 2022 on my business page! This was a goal I set in my heart and God fulfilled it. It's a small thing and yet a beautiful thing to know that He sees the desires of your heart even when they aren't things that impact eternity. A friend of mine recently shared how much LearningRx Shreveport had changed his life from a distance. You see, he sponsored a child to attend LearningRx Brain Training because the child attends church with him and could not read. The parents had done everything they could to help him but they lived in Texas not near a LearningRx center. This young man just wanted to read about hunting and his desire to read kept him motivated despite his age. At 11, boys especially who've been struggling a while usually become discouraged and become discipline problems but not the sweet kid. He got up extra early and met his personal trainer online remotely to brain train 3 days a week at 7am before school/chores. 6 months later he's a reading champ! This is my why!

So my friend who sponsored this kiddo spoke to my heart this past month and like Mary I have pondered what he said in my heart. He told me to remember the impact I was having on eternity through each brain we train. He told me of the impact that we had had on his life through the changes he sees in this young man. Brain training isn't just about changing one life...it has a ripple effect that goes on and on. It affects the family, the school setting and others around that one brain changed. My goal in 2022 is to train as many brains as possible, reach as many people as possible with God's love and to change lives one brain at a time because this is my marketplace of ministry. Thank you to all of you who support me! I invite you to be a small part of what we do. Go "like" LearningRx Shreveport business page to see great content about the brain and what we are doing, then invite your friends to like the page...it's as simple as the push of a button. There is someone out there that you know wanting or needing a lifeline that we provide. I'm proud to say I run my business with integrity and love. God has blessed me with this opportunity and I will use this missionfield to reach those in need.

He cares about your struggles in memory, attention, learning...He cares and He has called teachers to a passionate opportunity to help. Lord, thank you for seeing the desires of our heart and honoring us at LearningRx. We ask for your continued blessings and that each brain trained feels your presence in our center and see magnificent change in their lives. Allow the ripple effect to draw people to you.

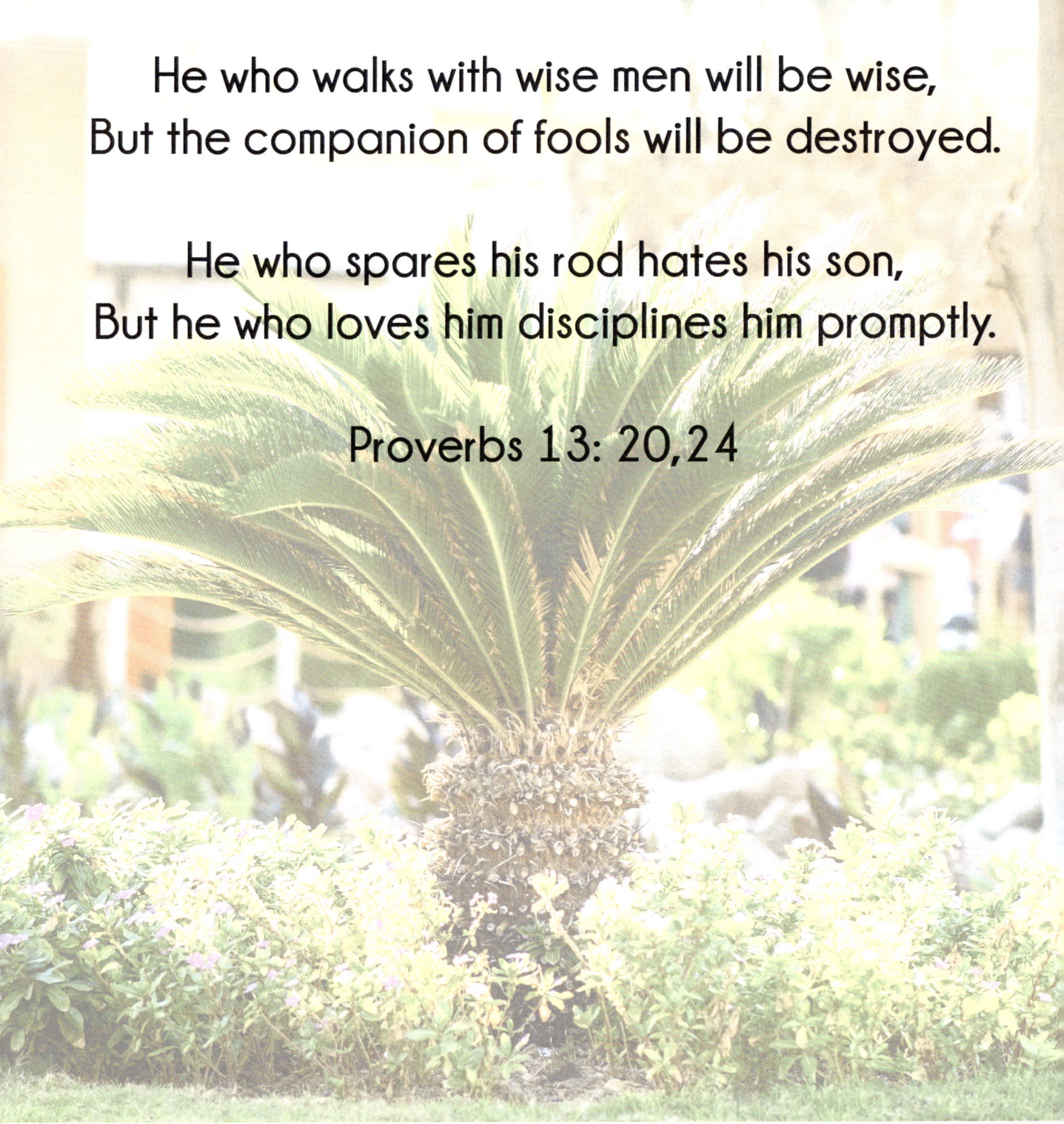

He who walks with wise men will be wise,
But the companion of fools will be destroyed.

He who spares his rod hates his son,
But he who loves him disciplines him promptly.

Proverbs 13: 20,24

Refusal To Love!

Two verses selected from the same chapter which is absolutely full of wise sayings. Idioms, verbal expressions and proverbs are all difficult for some people to interpret and this is a skill that is important. The key to learning to use wise words is by observation and relationships with those who are wise and reading...sometimes it's easy to get addicted to the videos and silliness on the net because some of it is too ridiculous for words. Anyway, Wes & I were watching a show when a commercial about paint or carpet came on showing these kids just making absolute chaos of the house...Wes commented that we never needed to replace paint/carpet because our kids knew better...we disciplined in love and constantly because the job of a parent is to correct and train a child in love. We are so proud of both our boys.

They have worked hard and accomplished much in just over 20 years of life. I could tout their successes but their failures are just as important, for it is in those moments of things not going well that they make me the proudest. Why? Because they use wisdom. They learned that mistakes don't derail you, they form you and help you grow. Things don't always go our way but we grow from the good and the bad. If there's always sunshine and never rain then a flower would wilt under the heat. When storms come, seek wisdom from those who have the strength and have weathered the storms. Discipline yourself as you discipline your child because in the training comes the wisdom. Lord, help me to be guided by your wisdom and not the fallacies of man.

You've all been to the stadium and seen the athletes race. Everyone runs; one wins. Run to win. All good athletes train hard. They do it for a gold medal that tarnishes and fades.
You're after one that's gold eternally.
I don't know about you, but I'm running hard for the finish line. I'm giving it everything I've got. No lazy living for me! I'm staying alert and in top condition. I'm not going to get caught napping, telling everyone else all about it and then missing out myself.

1 Corinthians 9: 24-27

Marathon of Life!

How are you running this marathon of life? Knowing that you win gold eternally if you run with all that's in you and run continuously should motivate you to push through. The Winter Olympics are starting soon and I think of all the years these athletes practice and prepare for that one run, that one downhill ski, that one jump, that one opportunity to make the gold and they aren't assured of the gold because only one will win it.

If we approached our lives as if we are reaching for the gold...working at loving and reaching people with all that is in us...knowing that our labor is not in vain and in fact we are guaranteed the prize of the high calling...if we did that, how our world would change. I know it's easy to get caught up in the aches and pains. It's easy to get trapped in the day to day but if we truly put our best effort in minute by minute...if we gave it our true best...if we would react in faith instead of unbelief...if we loved others even when they did us wrong...if we gave in love with all that we had...what a change we would make in this world.

I watched the snow change the landscape today. It was a light steady snow but the landscape changed almost magically...washed in white...somehow brighter than it was. The intricate details of each snowflake, lost in the mix but as they fell and combined their efforts...the landscape changed. Fall in love with Jesus again...run to Him and keep running this race of life...fellowship with other believers and bind together to change your landscape. It only takes a little effort to make a big difference in a life.

Lord, help me to be a kingdom shaker. Help me to be the difference in a life. Guide me in reaching others with your love and forgiveness. Let me use my time wisely for your glory. Mold me into the vessel you want me to be...a special individual like a snowflake that falls and becomes a magical change maker to the landscape of my life. Let me be your hands extended.

"In a word, what I'm saying is, Grow up. You're kingdom subjects. Now live like it. Live out your God-created identity. Live generously and graciously toward others, the way God lives toward you."

Matthew 5:48

Glial Growth!

The picture behind this scripture is a glial cell...a cell that connects other cells in the brain and stimulates them to grow! Growth only happens when it is stimulated or commanded by cells or by God or by training the cell to stimulate.
This scripture is Jesus saying "Grow up". Live as God designed you to live as He desires you to do, which is generously and graciously. Activating the cell can be done by training it to do its job. This is what a faith life is all about. Walk in faith and you walk out into kingdom-hood. If you walk in anger and frustration then you cause more anger and frustration to those around you but if you walk in belief, in faith, in God's provision then that is stimulating to others around you., Lord, please help me to walk in your love and live generously and graciously towards others around me. Show me your ways and wisdom and guide me in your paths of faith.

All praise to the God and Father of our Master, Jesus the Messiah! Father of all mercy! God of all healing counsel! He comes alongside us when we go through hard times, and before you know it, he brings us alongside someone else who is going through hard times so that we can be there for that person just as God was there for us. We have plenty of hard times that come from following the Messiah, but no more so than the good times of his healing comfort—we get a full measure of that, too.

2 Corinthians 1: 3-5

Purpose Through The Pain!

I am so grateful that God in His infinite wisdom brings healing and goes alongside us in hard times. When my mom went through the early part of her breast cancer journey, so many sweet people were there for us and we learned so much from others that helped us in that fight then as we learned we were able to help others as they went through their journeys. Through...my heart has been so encouraged this week by a little preposition THROUGH. God has purpose as He takes us Through this journey into the next place and it is Through this that we grow and learn so that we have purpose in helping others Through their journeys.

We are headed THROUGH to the full measure of His glory! Lord, let us see with new eyes your purpose and plan. Let us not get caught up in our place of struggling but rather focus on your purpose of taking us THROUGH the journey which is to be able to come alongside another as they walk Through to complete healing comfort for your glory! Anticipation of Complete Healing...miracles are happening as we believe!

I look up to the mountains;
does my strength come from mountains?
No, my strength comes from God,
who made heaven, and earth, and mountains.
He won't let you stumble,
your Guardian God won't fall asleep.
Not on your life! Israel's
Guardian will never doze or sleep.
God's your Guardian,
right at your side to protect you—
Shielding you from sunstroke,
sheltering you from moonstroke.
God guards you from every evil,
he guards your very life.
He guards you when you leave and when you return,
he guards you now, he guards you always.

Psalms 121: 1-8

Why Evil?

The magnificent and majestic mountains cannot help you in time of need. They cannot give you their strength nor lend you their majesty. But God, the creator of those same mountains does. He protects us, guards us, guides us and shields us many times unbeknownst to us. I hear a lot of questions about God from those who have hardships or struggles as I have had, wondering if God is so good, why then does pain & suffering happen to so many? Why is evil allowed? God created this world and man/woman chose to destroy the beauty He created by a selfish act...the human nature took hold. This is the truth that we avoid. God gives us free choice to choose to live in Him or to live without Him in our own selfishness.

Unfortunately too many choose the self and inflict their choices on others...this is sin. Looking into magnificent creation and nature, I can see God's hand in it daily. I celebrate that He is at work in our lives and He wants nothing but good for us. The choice is ours. We walk in His vision seeing that this is but a part of the journey in which He is with us or we walk in our own selfishness inflicting our will and choices on those around us. Lord, help me to walk in you and not in me!

"You're blessed when you feel you've lost what is most dear to you. Only then can you be embraced by the One most dear to you.
"You're blessed when you're content with just who you are— no more, no less. That's the moment you find yourselves proud owners of everything that can't be bought. "You're blessed when you've worked up a good appetite for God. He's food and drink in the best meal you'll ever eat.
"You're blessed when you care.
At the moment of being 'care-full,' you find yourselves cared for. "You're blessed when you get your inside world—your mind and heart—put right. Then you can see God in the outside world.
"You're blessed when you can show people how to cooperate instead of compete or fight. That's when you discover who you really are, and your place in God's family. "You're blessed when your commitment to God provokes persecution. The persecution drives you even deeper into God's kingdom.
"Not only that—count yourselves blessed every time people put you down or throw you out or speak lies about you to discredit me. What it means is that the truth is too close for comfort and they are uncomfortable. You can be glad when that happens—give a cheer, even!
- for though they don't like it, I do!
And all heaven applauds. And know that you are in good company. My prophets and witnesses have always gotten into this kind of trouble.

Matthew 5: 4-12

Perspectives!

Perspective is a small thing that really matters in photos and life! I used the same photo to highlight all these scriptures because God is telling us through these that our blessings don't always come as things we like but rather as perspective that grows us into the person He desires us to be.
Be blessed today. Look through His eyes of eternity and see His heart. Lord, help me to not get caught up in the day to day but to keep my eyes on you so that my perspective sees each moment as a blessing from you!

What marvelous love the Father has extended to us! Just look at it—we're called children of God! That's who we really are. But that's also why the world doesn't recognize us or take us seriously, because it has no idea who he is or what he's up to. But friends, that's exactly who we are: children of God. And that's only the beginning. Who knows how we'll end up! What we know is that when Christ is openly revealed, we'll see him—and in seeing him, become like him. All of us who look forward to his Coming stay ready, with the glistening purity of Jesus' life as a model for our own.

1 John 3: 1-3

Uniqueness!

I love uniqueness and in this world that our Father created there is so much unique beauty from these colorful birds to the painted skies. The intricate details of our world fascinate me. But even more, what a crazy fantastic love that God has for us, his creation. We are His children! We are often not recognized or taken seriously for that but we have His authority to operate in the unseen on this earth through Him! Jesus came as an example of a pure life to us and He sacrificed that spotless life to become the ultimate Lamb of God delivering us from the wages of sin and into eternal life. We have only to accept His gift and walk in it. I know many people who accept a gift who then put the gift in the closet never using it, never thinking about it. How disturbing and disappointing is it that this gift is accepted by many and discarded just as quickly without truly understanding the value of this intangible offering. We are His.

The sheep of His pasture. The heirs to His kingdom. The bride of Christ. We have an important role to play in His creation and we need to understand and embrace this. Lord, help me to step up to what you have for me. Help me to be all that you have for me with my uniqueness of talents and abilities. Let me be used by you to be your hands extended.

A good man out of the good treasure of his heart brings forth good; and an evil man out of the evil treasure of his heart brings forth evil. For out of the abundance of the heart his mouth speaks.

Luke 6:45

Hot Air!

I love seeing hot air balloons flying as it is fascinating to me. They are dependent on the winds catching them to move across the sky yet they have control of their lift by the amount of heat they use in the balloon. I don't understand all the principles of it but I have some friends who do and who even write about it. What is flying your balloon of life? The scripture says it is what is in abundance in your heart. Many people wonder about how such evil can come from those currently in charge of our government...evil breeds evil and good breeds good. What you fill your heart with pours out of you especially in times of stress and hard situations. The mouth pours out what the heart is filled with daily.

What are you filling up with? Are you drinking from the living water or the stagnant pools of the flesh? Lord, I thank you that you refresh us daily with your living waters that satisfies our every need. I thank you that you provide for us before we think to ask. I humbly ask you to refresh me with your presence so that my heart is satisfied with your constancy. Help me to be all that you would have me to be and to pour out of my mouth all that you would have me to speak. Purify me so that beauty and goodness fill me so others might see and be blessed.

Do not love the world or the things in the world. If anyone loves the world, the love of the Father is not in him. For all that is in the world—the lust of the flesh, the lust of the eyes, and the pride of life—is not of the Father but is of the world. And the world is passing away, and the lust of it; but he who does the will of God abides forever.

1 John 2: 15-17

Too Much!

You cannot drive down the road or flip on TV, radio, or the internet without being bombarded by things! Advertising is everywhere and as a business owner it makes my heart glad but as a Christ follower, it makes me cringe at the encouraging lust of the flesh and of the eye that is targeting our every waking moment. How then can one be other than desirous of these things. We become full as a tick bloated in things so that we have to get storage buildings to hold the things we own but never or rarely use. The world as we know it is ever changing and passing away but the things that are eternal can be laid up in Heaven where neither time nor thieves can destroy. Lord, help me to focus on things above and rid myself of the pride of life and lusts of this world. Keep my eyes fixed on you!

Now godliness with contentment is great gain. For we brought nothing into this world, and it is certain we can carry nothing out. And having food and clothing, with these we shall be content. But those who desire to be rich fall into temptation and a snare, and into many foolish and harmful lusts which drown men in destruction and perdition. For the love of money is a root of all kinds of evil, for which some have strayed from the faith in their greediness, and pierced themselves through with many sorrows.

Timothy 6: 6-10

Rooted!

I've always been fascinated by the cypress tree. It thrives in the water and the roots travel huge distances connecting together to provide stability to each other...many a boater has made the mistake of getting in too close and becoming bound up in that root system. Spanish moss hangs symbiotically from the branches and gives a ghostly beauty to them. Godliness is like the cypress in that the root system is strongly intertwined with contentment. You have to know in whom you have believed and be persuaded that no matter what, he's got your back. You have to KNOW! Contentment is the opposite of Contention. They both have the same base but very different meanings and many times we allow our roots to become entangled with other things that drift by in life stacking up in our system and bogging down our life flow causing our contentment to become contentiousness. Today is a day I choose to clean the clogs around my root system by allowing God to lead me back to the Life giving flow of His peace. It is a choice!

You can choose to be content no matter your circumstances or you can choose to be contentious! Believe me, the people around you know where you are drinking and if your life flow is clogged! Lord, thank you that you see me and know me more than myself. Clear my life flow Lord. Take away the dross that weighs me down and allow me to reflect your beauty and contentment. Help me to be the person you desire me to be in all things!

If then you were raised with Christ, seek those things which are above, where Christ is, sitting at the right hand of God. Set your mind on things above, not on things on the earth.
But now you yourselves are to put off all these: anger, wrath, malice, blasphemy, filthy language out of your mouth. Do not lie to one another, since you have put off the old man with his deeds, and have put on the new man who is renewed in knowledge according to the image of Him who created him,

Colossians 3: 1-2, 8-10

What Are You Seeking?

Wealth? Fame? Kindness? Self-control? God? Things? What are your priorities? God tells us to seek those things above...so what are those things? What should we set our mind on in order to not be trapped and bogged down by the things of earth that He tells us to put off? The heavenly things... the eternal promises...the blessed hope...the love of God...the peace that passes all understanding...the faith the moves mountains and sees miracles here in the earthly realm. He tells us to put on the new man who is renewed in knowledge according to the image of Him who created us. That means that our eyes should be set on Him so that our vision is refocused through the lens of His love, His image, His sight. Lord, today I thank you that you are here with us ready to direct us for your glory as we set our minds on you. I ask you to help me to see through your vision.

Take the scales of earthly weights off my eyes and help me to see with heavenly eyes all that you are doing. Give me your vision for the future and direct my steps so I may seek what you would have me to seek and not get caught up in the pettiness. I thank you that you give us the ability to see you and hear you through your Holy Spirit and your word. Guide me today in your presence.

You shall love the Lord your God with all your heart, with all your soul, and with all your strength. "And these words which I command you today shall be in your heart. You shall teach them diligently to your children, and shall talk of them when you sit in your house, when you walk by the way, when you lie down, and when you rise up. You shall bind them as a sign on your hand, and they shall be as frontlets between your eyes. You shall write them on the doorposts of your house and on your gates.

Deuteronomy 6: 5-9

The Great Commandment!

The great commandment which solves all earth's ills but yet many do the opposite. It doesn't say you should not, you can not nor it would be best for you but you SHALL. Shall is a strong intention..it means you intentionally do it...not accidentally nor half heartedly. Just think of how different our world would be if we intentionally and purposefully did these things...taught these principles diligently to our kids, talked of them at the dinner table, as we visit in our living rooms and at social events, as we walk through our day at work with coworkers and as we get ready for bed...every morning as we get going...we intentionally loved with all that is in us and we were full of God's love....what if we intentionally wrote them on our doors & gates...what if....wait a minute...that's how our country was founded...I think we need to get back to God's love...put our selfish ways aside and begin to prioritize His love once again...it's our mission, our purpose in life.

For His anger is but for a moment,
His favor is for life;
Weeping may endure for a night,
But joy comes in the morning.

Psalms 30:5

Your Plan!

Many loved ones have gone before us in these last couple of years unjustly and many too early which has made us as a people and country stay in a state of grief and anguish, anxiety and fear. God doesn't want this for us. He wants us to look to the dawn and realize that there is joy on the horizon if we will but put our hand in His and completely trust. Weeping cleanses us when it is for a season as it washes the eyes. Lord, help us to see you in the dawn and in the day. Help us to trust in your plan.

Do not let your adornment be merely outward— arranging the hair, wearing gold, or putting on fine apparel— rather let it be the hidden person of the heart, with the incorruptible beauty of a gentle and quiet spirit, which is very precious in the sight of God.

For "He who would love life And see good days,
Let him refrain his tongue from evil,
And his lips from speaking deceit.
Let him turn away from evil and do good;
Let him seek peace and pursue it.
For the eyes of the Lord are on the righteous,
And His ears are open to their prayers;
But the face of the Lord is against
those who do evil."

1 Peter 3: 3-4, 10-12

Beauty!

The incorruptible beauty of the quiet and gentle spirits marching today for the Right to Life were very precious in God's sight. It wasn't a bunch of inappropriate headdresses and a big production of pomp but rather a peaceful pursuit of righteousness which God saw and turned His eyes toward. Do not be fooled...the heresy of those who choose to steal the life of the unborn has raised a stink in the nostrils of God and the evil words/rhetoric which fills the news channels are abhorrent to Him. Today is a day to honor the sanctity of life for the unborn.

"Therefore do not worry, saying, 'What shall we eat?' or 'What shall we drink?' or 'What shall we wear?' For after all these things the Gentiles seek. For your heavenly Father knows that you need all these things. But seek first the kingdom of God and His righteousness, and all these things shall be added to you. Therefore do not worry about tomorrow, for tomorrow will worry about its own things. Sufficient for the day is its own trouble.

Matthew 6: 31-34

Leaning In!

Breanna Ponder used to sing a song at church that really portrayed this for me...I still picture that sweet young lady as she sang the words...I just want to rest upon Jesus and trust Him...I just want to lay back on Him and know He's got it all. Breathe deep and trust in Him. Some days my stress and tension level are so high that it is exhausting and on those days I've got to remember to lean in on Him. Lord, help me to feel you and not be so stressed. Help me to simply trust and not stress. Help me not to worry but rather to seek your face and your kingdom first.

"I want to lean back against you and breathe, feel your heartbeat. Your love is so deep, it's more than I can stand. I melt in your peace, it's overwhelming"

The heavens declare the glory of God;
And the firmament shows His handiwork.
Day unto day utters speech,
And night unto night reveals knowledge.
There is no speech nor language
Where their voice is not heard.
Their line has gone out through all the earth,
And their words to the end of the world.
In them He has set a tabernacle for the sun,
Which is like a bridegroom coming out of his chamber,
And rejoices like a strong man to run its race.
Its rising is from one end of heaven,
And its circuit to the other end;
And there is nothing hidden from its heat.

Psalms 19: 1-6

Pondering!

Sitting here pondering things...fascinated with the beautiful moon and night sky...thinking of all the things He has done. Things are somewhat frustrating right now for me as I want to be 100% but keep getting hit with setbacks...the latest of which is blood clots and varicose veins causing bad swelling in my legs. Life and all the challenges that come can sometimes wear one out...but I am so grateful to look at these skies and see that He is still in control. The Chinese may want to control the weather and have machines to manipulate it but the reality is they don't have control just as no one in our government actually has a say so. It would drive them crazy to hear that but it's the truth. No matter what happens, I know who holds my future. He created it and me. He created the heavens, the earth and all else. We struggle so hard sometimes to simply come to the realization that it's all about Him....why should I worry, stress and freak when He's got this? I need to just practice my deep breathing and leaning in.

The more I struggle against it, the more the weights of life tighten around me but when I relax in Him...they just fall away. I will still follow doctor's orders to an extent that wisdom dictates but I know The Great Physician. He's on time. I just need to get to the proper waiting room so that He can see me and I can see/hear Him. I appreciate any prayers for a complete touch and I also ask for my mom who needs some answers too. Genetically speaking...I am her child so she is having some of the same issues but just doesn't say anything. Pray for God to touch her feet/legs also. Lord, I am so grateful for the beauty of your presence in my everyday life and how you demonstrate your care for me in the skies themselves. What a wonder you are My Great Creator and My Great Physician. How blessed am I that you think enough of me to light the sky in wonder. I come to you humbly asking for intervention in my situation and that of my mom. Please move as only you can do, giving wisdom, guidance and complete healing for it is by the stripes upon Jesus' back that we claim our healing. He bore those so that we might be healed. I thank you for your healing touch and I will walk in faith knowing that you have all things working for my good and for the good of my mom and for your kingdom. Thank you for your precious sacrifice and the opportunity to come to you with these needs.

But may the God of all grace, who called us to His eternal glory by Christ Jesus, after you have suffered a while, perfect, establish, strengthen, and settle you.

1 Peter 5:10

Timelines!

I must confess that my timeline and God's don't always align but I was completely encouraged this morning by this verse because the suffering for a little while has definitely been happening! I am ready to be perfected, established, strengthened and settled. I am ready to feel better. This journey isn't for the light of heart at all. We have been called to His purpose...His eternal glory...with His grace...everything is going to be alright!

O Lord, You have searched me and known me. You know my sitting down and my rising up;
You understand my thought afar off. You comprehend my path and my lying down,
And are acquainted with all my ways. For there is not a word on my tongue,
But behold, O Lord, You know it altogether. You have hedged me behind and before,
And laid Your hand upon me. Such knowledge is too wonderful for me;
It is high, I cannot attain it. Where can I go from Your Spirit?
Or where can I flee from Your presence? If I ascend into heaven, You are there;
If I make my bed in hell, behold, You are there. If I take the wings of the morning,
And dwell in the uttermost parts of the sea, Even there Your hand shall lead me,
And Your right hand shall hold me. If I say, "Surely the darkness shall fall on me,"
Even the night shall be light about me; Indeed, the darkness shall not hide from You,
But the night shines as the day; The darkness and the light are both alike to You.
For You formed my inward parts; You covered me in my mother's womb.
I will praise You, for I am fearfully and wonderfully made;
Marvelous are Your works, And that my soul knows very well.
My frame was not hidden from You, When I was made in secret,
And skillfully wrought in the lowest parts of the earth.
Your eyes saw my substance, being yet unformed. And in Your book they all were written,
The days fashioned for me, When as yet there were none of them.
How precious also are Your thoughts to me, O God! How great is the sum of them!
If I should count them, they would be more in number than the sand;
When I awake, I am still with You. Oh, that You would slay the wicked, O God!
Depart from me, therefore, you bloodthirsty men. For they speak against You wickedly;
Your enemies take Your name in vain. Do I not hate them, O Lord, who hate You?
And do I not loathe those who rise up against You? I hate them with perfect hatred;
I count them my enemies. Search me, O God, and know my heart;
Try me, and know my anxieties; And see if there is any wicked way in me,
And lead me in the way everlasting.

Psalms 139: 1-24

Better Than Chocolate!

Psalms 139 is a beautiful song of how God understands us...who we are, where we are going, what we need more than we do. It is a refreshing collection of verses that lift the spirit and encourage us to rest in his Omnipotence. Oh how great His love is for us. A chapter in pictures....because I couldn't choose just a verse today. So much richness it was like choosing the best piece of chocolate in a bowl of chocolates. Taste & see that God is good today...better than a box of chocolates!

So we are always confident, knowing that while we are at home in the body we are absent from the Lord. For we walk by faith, not by sight. We are confident, yes, well pleased rather to be absent from the body and to be present with the Lord.

Therefore, if anyone is in Christ, he is a new creation; old things have passed away; behold, all things have become new.

2 Corinthians 5: 6-8, 17

Outer Vessel!

I read a series from Ted Dekker years ago that struck me so. When the character in the book slept he awoke in another realm. His body on earth was resting but His spirit was in battle in the other realm and He warred fiercely until he decided to rest...when he rested in the spirit, his earthly body awoke. There is a veil that keeps us from seeing and knowing all that is happening but I truly believe that we are continually fighting a spiritual war and it takes a toll on our physical beings. This body is not my eternal home...I'm not even that attached to it with all its flaws but I care for it as the temple of God because I know His Spirit dwells in me. I don't get caught up in a lotta drama with fads on clothes, etc...I just wear what I like. I hear people comment on the outer person often...weight, beauty, blah, blah...what I would rather hear is what I heard yesterday when I stopped in a store to grab a drink and the girl said, "wait, can you pray with me because I see the light in you and I know God hears you!" Folks, that is the best compliment ever.

    She saw my Father in me...shining through me as I did an everyday errand on a mundane day...the seams of the fabric holding the veil are being permeated....people are hungry for REAL and not false...they want Truth. So here's my question today? Will you spend enough time with him to fill up to overflowing so that you can spill a little at your normal errands? Can you overtop enough that it catches onto a coworker? Lord, I thank you for your effervescent joy that bubbles and overtops any situation when we rest in you. Please let my life be used up for you. It is my desire to be aware of your presence everywhere and walk in fullness. I see the seams of the veil you are wearing and Lord I am ready to be a vessel for your service.

Lift up your heads, O you gates!
And be lifted up, you everlasting doors!
And the King of glory shall come in.
Who is this King of glory?
The Lord strong and mighty,
The Lord mighty in battle.
Lift up your heads, O you gates!
Lift up, you everlasting doors!
And the King of glory shall come in.
Who is this King of glory?
The Lord of hosts,
He is the King of glory.
Selah

Psalms 24: 7-10

Gate Opener!

I've never pictured myself as a gate/door but David is drawing a symbolic picture here of the ability of our hearts/minds to decide to look up and celebrate the King of Glory... to open our hearts & minds in celebration of who He is. He is challenging us to get out of our circumstances and choose to look up with the eyes of wonder realizing that the King of Glory...the creator of all, desires to come dwell in us. He can do the battle for you. He is strong & mighty....He is the King...will you lift up the gates and open the everlasting doors of your heart to begin to see the King of Glory move on your behalf?

Lord, today I lift the gates of my eyes that have been shuttered to your mightiness protecting what I could see instead of opening and seeing your mighty glory. I throw open the gates of my heart so I can stretch my faith and believe that the mighty King of Glory will come in to work a supreme work in my life. Today I will dine with you in your presence on fullness of joy. I will eat the fruits of your mercy & grace and drink the ambrosia of the fruits of your spirit. Today I lift up my head to realize & see that you and only you reign!

Therefore the prudent keep silent at that time, For it is an evil time.
Seek good and not evil,
That you may live;
So the Lord God of hosts will be with you,
As you have spoken.
Hate evil, love good;
Establish justice in the gate.
It may be that the Lord God of hosts
Will be gracious to the remnant of Joseph.

Amos 5: 13-15

Prudence!

Amos, the prophet of God, was foretelling times ahead to the people warning them that God was tired of tolerating their complete disdain. I feel this is where we are now at as a country. God has allowed this evil to prevail long enough. He is instructing through Amos for those who still follow Him to be thoughtfully careful (prudent)...choosing your words wisely and who you share them with carefully. The lesson for us is to be wise as serpents and harmless as doves as we approach others for we do not know the exact timing of His return but we do know it is soon and the closer it gets, the more evil will reveal itself. Satan knows his time is at an end and he runs around wreaking havoc everywhere he can.

"O Jerusalem, Jerusalem, the one who kills the prophets and stones those who are sent to her! How often I wanted to gather your children together, as a hen gathers her chicks under her wings, but you were not willing!

Matthew 23:37

Substitutions!

Let's play substitution...and put America in the place of Jerusalem. Have we as a country done everything in our power to refuse God access to our kids by pulling them away continuously from idle things? Are we prioritizing Him above other things or are we too busy tearing down the church and Godly principles in front of them? Recently I watched a friend who is on fire for God and excited about what He is doing get throttled by people on FB for promoting revival? Why? Because of fear that it will change our city for the better. Oh they used words like "CoVid" and social distancing but I can tell you that her hunger isn't diminished but God's work In those people's lives is...not because of Him or her but because of them. Oh be careful my friends that today we do not shut down what God is doing because it looks different than what you are used to seeing. Now try your name, personalize it...

Oh, Donesa, are you one who kills the prophet and stones those sent by your actions, deeds? Donesa, are you willingly keeping your children from the house of God? Allowing other things to take the place of importance in your home? Father, forgive me for where I have failed you! Help me to reprioritize and get back to my first love.

that we should no longer be children, tossed to and fro and carried about with every wind of doctrine, by the trickery of men, in the cunning craftiness of deceitful plotting, but, speaking the truth in love, may grow up in all things into Him who is the head—Christ— from whom the whole body, joined and knit together by what every joint supplies, according to the effective working by which every part does its share, causes growth of the body for the edifying of itself in love.

Ephesians 4: 14-16

Knit Together!

Paul instructs the church at Ephesians to work together as a body to support one another because it is important to the whole. There are so many times in history that the tide of history would have changed had the church been functioning as a body instead of muscle groups against each other. Since my back surgery, I have been unable to sleep very much because of the aches and sore muscles. My weak muscles pull against others then constrict and I cannot get them to relax… which then causes tension in others which then results in pain… suffice it to say that the body has suffered an injury and is reacting angrily. I started PT to help these muscles and joints, tendons, etc to learn to relax again. We are the bride of Christ and as such must function as one body to be what Christ desires us to be but do not be deceived…this isn't the same as one world religion which the Antichrist spirit is putting forth now.

The bride knows her place, her role and her function. We aren't children to be misled but rather a functioning body of believers. If you are not plugged into an actively growing and living church, come join me at our church where God is moving.

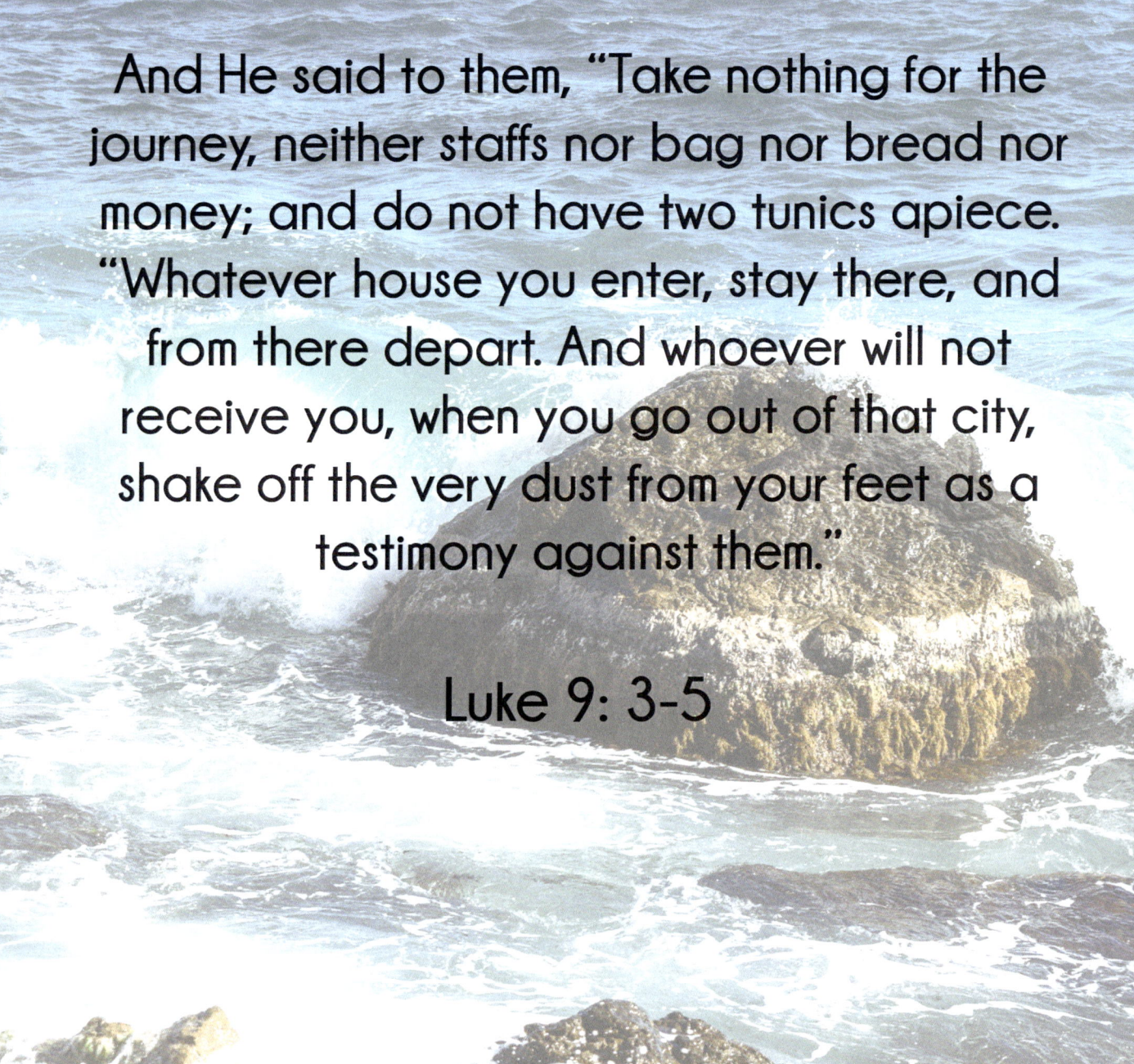

And He said to them, "Take nothing for the journey, neither staffs nor bag nor bread nor money; and do not have two tunics apiece. "Whatever house you enter, stay there, and from there depart. And whoever will not receive you, when you go out of that city, shake off the very dust from your feet as a testimony against them."

Luke 9: 3-5

Contingency!

What a powerful word in this day of planning for every contingency! Our God shall supply all our needs…& yet we get so caught up in the planning of tomorrow that we fail to plan for eternity. I am so blessed and yet often I fail to realize this and instead get caught up in the "if onlys". Jesus is instructing us to not be so full of care of this world that we neglect the purpose of this journey. Lord, help me to see your purpose before all else and not be caught up in the whims of the current trends and desires. Help me to keep my eyes focused on the prize of the highest calling!

For if we have been united together in the likeness of His death, certainly we also shall be in the likeness of His resurrection, knowing this, that our old man was crucified with Him, that the body of sin might be done away with, that we should no longer be slaves of sin. For he who has died has been freed from sin.

Romans 6: 5-7

Warning: This Is A Sermon!!!

What a powerful mindset of peace when those who live in Christ actually absorb this truth: Death no longer has control or any reign in your life! Wow! I mean getting old stinks. The body, this earthly frame begins dying the moment we are born and despite the miracle of neurogenesis, we are losing more cells than we are making by our early 30s. And 50...well, let's just say I had 4 major illnesses resulting in surgery for 3 of them. We work hard to maintain this fragile frame of dust through diet, exercise of both brain and body and all the cosmetic help....but if we have learned one thing in the last few years, it's that life is fragile. We cannot control what happens to our bodies all the time...although we can give it the best chance. We cannot control death nor the grave but we can walk in victory over both, boldly without fear because Jesus Christ conquered both.

What I am saying now will make some people mad...because the truth hurts...if you claim to be a Christian and walk in FEAR of death then you are walking on the shoulder or gravel of the road or skidding off. I don't care what your situation is nor your opinion on vaccines nor your political stance. To the true believer, FEAR of death is a sin. Ouch! Why? Because Christ conquered death and the fear of it and the grave and the sin that weighs all of it. I know many people refusing to go to church because they feel it has become a "death trap" or "too political". At risk of offending those people...the truth is that if this is you, you are walking in FEAR and LIES which is a cloud of SIN!

When you are truly saved, you walk with Christ who conquered all these. Does this mean you don't use sense or treat your failing body with medications, interventions, surgeries, etc? Of course not...these are things that God has allowed & created to help this temporary frame. Do you make plans for death in case it comes? Sure. I have a thorough plan with letters for my family and my last will written. These are tools to assist you in conquering the unknown because that is where the fear lies. I'll be very frank. I haven't ever feared death but I

Now if we died with Christ, we believe that we shall also live with Him, knowing that Christ, having been raised from the dead, dies no more. Death no longer has dominion over Him. For the death that He died, He died to sin once for all; but the life that He lives, He lives to God. Likewise you also, reckon yourselves to be dead indeed to sin, but alive to God in Christ Jesus our Lord.

Romans 6: 8-11

have worried over how my passing could affect my family, friends, business and made plans to assist if & when death occurs. There is nothing more awful than watching the transition from life to death for an unbeliever who fears death...it's worse than that scene from "Ghosts". On the other hand, the transition from this life to the next for a believer who is walking in complete peace is amazingly beautiful. The death part isn't always pretty as the body is often ravaged but the peace part is, as many times they see a loved one or Jesus himself.

Why am I expounding on this so much? The church, the bride of Christ has been unfaithful...allowing the media and the scientific & political community to clothe her in a robe of fear obscuring the light of life.

We are not called to a spirit of fear but one of life, love & happiness. Our spirit is contagious when we walk in Him. Our confidence and our hope is fully in Him. When we have truly laid down our mortal for His immortality, we are no longer weighted by the fear of death but rather we are raised into His likeness in resurrection! Jesus Christ, the king of all glory died on a cross in the most awful way so that you can walk in freedom of life. Quit walking around as a poor me! Get your head up! Quit allowing fear to cloak His light. Cast off those heavy outer garments the world has shrouded you in Church! You are the Bride of the king of Kings! You walk in miracles! You walk in beauty, peace and fruit of the Spirit! You dwell in power and have Dominion over all the Earth with His authority! It's time that the church-the bride wakes up!

Relight your lamp! Reignite your fire, your passion, your love once again! You aren't a slave to sin or this world with its dredges! Live like you are the Queen of Glory...not in falseness but in truth. Shake off those heavy bands...lift up those Holy hands! Grace! God's grace...unmerited favor!

Therefore do not let sin reign in your mortal body, that you should obey it in its lusts. And do not present your members as instruments of unrighteousness to sin, but present yourselves to God as being alive from the dead, and your members as instruments of righteousness to God. For sin shall not have dominion over you, for you are not under law but under grace.

Romans 6: 12-14

Lord, forgive us for allowing the weight of sin and the cloak of darkness to shroud your light in our lives. Forgive us for hearing the report of the doctor and failing to trust that you have all things in your hand and in your time. Forgive us Lord for allowing fear to reign over our households keeping us from fellowshipping with the saints and allowing the weight of fear of death to hold us in place instead of running the race of the true believers. Lord, we know you conquered death, fear, and the grave. We know that you are much greater than any talking head on the TV or social media. We know that you are Supreme. We ask that you reign Supreme in our lives. Father, we bind this evil that is flooding our world and we walk in your authority over it in our lives. Quicken our spirits, Lord to begin to clean up our dusty corners and shake off the heavy weights that have held us stagnant too long.

Give us your peace that passes all understanding that we may thrive and walk in confidence in your grace! Make us your vessels of miracles of healing and restoration! We know the end of times is near and the harvest is ready. Send us as laborers filled with the fire of your spirit to our mission fields, our workplaces, our homes, our socializations... allow us to be a reflection of your light that cannot be quenched by the passing cloud nor eclipsed by the objects or people around us. For we your people are humbling ourselves to you now in repentance asking for your glory to yet reign in our lives! We will be your bride adorned only for your glory once again!

Pile your troubles on God's shoulders—
he'll carry your load, he'll help you out.
He'll never let good people
topple into ruin.
But you, God, will throw the others
into a muddy bog,
Cut the lifespan of assassins
and traitors in half.
And I trust in you.

Psalms 55: 22-23

Pile Up!

    This picture made me smile as I thought of the penguins choosing this particular iceberg to shelter and rest on. The sides are steep and not in the sun. It's a slippery slope but perhaps that's why they chose it. I couldn't help but think of how we are so in need of certainty that we fail to realize that God has got this and all we have to do is trust. Yes, it may be out of the sunshine right now and even appear to be a slippery surface but for sure He knows the reason. Maybe the slippery slope is so that we can have some fun in life or maybe it is so we can strengthen and stretch our faith. Perhaps the struggle is because we are trying to carry too much rather than trusting Him with the load. Lord, whatever my circumstances today...I trust in you. Although it may appear slippery and even cold, out of the warmth of certainty...I will trust in you! You are my provider, my shield, my shelter and my all. I will trust in you!

Now may He who supplies seed to the sower, and bread for food, supply and multiply the seed you have sown and increase the fruits of your righteousness, while you are enriched in everything for all liberality, which causes thanksgiving through us to God.

Thanks be to God for His indescribable gift!

2 Corinthians 9: 10-11, 15

Thankful Heart!

What causes a thankful heart? Does getting everything you want without effort or laboring and achievement? The truth is that a caterpillar never becomes a butterfly until she labors to escape the cocoon because by doing so she strengthens the mechanisms in her system needed for flight. A seed must go into the ground and have a season of breaking open and stretching through the dark, dank ground to reach the sun and grow to produce fruit & flowers. All of us have processes that must take place in our lives in order to grow but the most important is the realization that gratitude or a thankful heart comes from the hard places. My goal this year is to be thankful in all things which means that I have some growth going to happen this year. I am going to count my blessings and my struggles that will become places of gratefulness. I am going to remember that God is the one who supplies my needs according to His riches in glory and I refuse to allow the storms of life to steal my joy. I am setting my heart towards an attitude of gratitude and growing in Him!

My brethren, count it all joy when you fall into various trials, knowing that the testing of your faith produces patience. But let patience have its perfect work, that you may be perfect and complete, lacking nothing. If any of you lacks wisdom, let him ask of God, who gives to all liberally and without reproach, and it will be given to him. But let him ask in faith, with no doubting, for he who doubts is like a wave of the sea driven and tossed by the wind. For let not that man suppose that he will receive anything from the Lord; he is a double-minded man, unstable in all his ways.

James 1: 2-8

A Worry Through!

    Yesterday in church, a word of wisdom and knowledge from the Lord came and said very clearly that He is taking us THROUGH the trials and tests so that we may reap the harvest of souls with him for through our tests we become more like Him and are able to understand those who are struggling.

    A couple of weeks ago, I had a vision of a girl in our church in a bridal gown walking through an outpouring (a physical blue tunnel pouring from Heaven into the church) of God's spirit in our church as people from different walks of my life (colleagues, church family, etc) stood around praying as the voice of God spoke clearly saying "Restoration", then another young man rolled through the tunnel in his wheelchair and walked out the other side as the voice said "miraculous healings" and there was a long line of people waiting to come in the doors.
The next day I got a group text of this same woman in that exact dress by "accident". I didn't know she wasn't married and is getting married in February.

    I got chills thinking that God is about to do something amazing here in Shreveport. I've been praying daily for this city and for an outpouring of His spirit upon us. It's time for us to Rise Up in faith believing and quit "worrying through our prayers". Time for boldness and believing without a second thought as to whether God will do it. He wants us to be whole! Why am I telling you this? Yesterday, I laid hands on my legs and prayed to the Great Physician to do what only He can do. I felt the clots begin to dissolve. They are not all gone yet but a work is happening in my body. I was almost pain free yesterday and it was a very busy day! I am so excited that our God is faithful! Yes, I am on meds and following doctor's orders and yes those meds are a part of this process but God is the key. He holds it all in His hands. I don't know what I'm doing but I pray to Him and He helps me, directs me, leads me. Lord, I am so grateful that you are a God of promises that are true and trustworthy! Thank you for touching my life and my body. Help me to be a part of this great awakening you have prepared for me.

Rejoice in the Lord always. Again I will say, rejoice! Let your gentleness be known to all men. The Lord is at hand.

Not that I speak in regard to need, for I have learned in whatever state I am, to be content:

I can do all things through Christ who strengthens me.

And my God shall supply all your need according to His riches in glory by Christ Jesus.

Philippians 4: 4-5, 11, 13, 19

Steady Rejoicing!

Philippians 4 is quite the letter from Paul to the church at Philippi. These 3 verses are just a few of the ones I hear often taken from context and used to further agendas. People always do that to assure themselves. Let me assure you that rejoicing in the Lord does open the floodgates of heaven in your situation…but rejoicing happens in all situations not just when things are going your way…rejoicing is a state of mind/heart where one chooses to be content and involved in fellowship/relationship. Yes, we can do all things through Christ but we must first learn these principles of thanksgiving and blessings in all situations.

God does supply all our needs (and some of our wants too) but you must be aligned to His purpose and in relationship. These verses like all verses in scripture have power. Read the chapter and realize that Paul was exhorting the church to establish a firmly rooted relationship in Christ that nothing could shake. This type of rooting gives us strength and purpose. Lord, let me be rooted in you this year. Unshaken by the happenings around me and in my world. Steady and trusting in who you are and who I am in you. Make my life a living sacrifice, totally devoted to you so I might be what you desire me to be.